The Unfinished Family

Barbara E. Murphy

Červená Barva Press
Somerville, Massachusetts

Červená Barva Press
P.O. Box 440357
W. Somerville, MA 02144

www.cervenabarvapress.com

Bookstore: www.thelostbookshelf.com

Production: Allison O'Keefe

ISBN: 978-1-950063-92-5

Library of Congress Control Number: 2024935835

For Tom, bravest of us all
and Tate, Stella, Rudy.
Already perfect

O mother and father I prematurely grieved,
Where are you now that I need to lose you?

—*Maggie Anderson*

CONTENTS

I.

II.

III.

The
Unfinished
Family

I.

When the Girls Were Girls

for Nancy

We should have taken
bigger steps
made deeper ruts
written longer poems.

When we wept over our
betraying lovers—
who returned, as we knew
they would,
to their wives, their dens
and afternoon naps—
you said we never really
wanted them. We wanted
their lives, their hours
at the desk,
their finished books.

We fit ourselves
into smaller and smaller places,
dressed in black,
more glimpsed than seen.
We did not mean
to take up so little space.

Learning to Be New

We thought we were over
telling stories, joking
at ourselves, heroes
of our own adventures.
But just last season
when a wind pushed east
out of somewhere toward us
who should know better
by now—no spare batteries,
candles burned down
to half-inch stumps—
we just shrugged. The couple
across the street, they
of the tidy yard and matching lycra,
are firing up the generator, packing
the car for possible evacuation.

But we surprised ourselves
when, in the damp cellar,
we unearthed two rusty headlamps
that worked! We high-fived,
and bumping our way upstairs,
practiced blinking them
on and off, crawled forward
as if through caves, taking a chance
on the faint light ahead.

Late Hike in Winter

Shouldn't we have packed a change
of socks, told someone

we were headed into sketchy
cell phone territory?

Our pole tips spear mud-stuck
bronzed leaves, slush

in frozen pewter folds as if
the wind had stopped mid-sentence.

Enough freeze to turn
the trail dry-ice silver.

I don't mean to be charging ahead
arms pumping, heart double-timing.

Stillness is not an arrow
in my late-life quiver.

We squint to keep each other in sight.
One waits for the other
where the trail divides.

Naming the Waterbirds

For Tom

There, on a narrow point
of ice, a pine needle's breadth
from the barely thawed river.

Merganser, I say
not because I know
but because I love

the sounds, the hushed z's
of organza, orgasmic. No,
my birder husband corrects me,

mallard—
sledge hammer of a word
I hear as *mallet*.

Oblivious, the duck stays,
as we do, near, still
on this immeasurable azure day.

Our Quiet Spring

For Judith

Through a thick winter window
I stare at a locust tree—
willing it to bud, to perform
exactly as it did last year,
the twenty before that, transfiguring
that pale, shaky spring
into broad spectrum summer.

How could we have known
that this season
would want only
simple acts? a knock
at the neighbor's door
with a pot of soup, a handful
of still damp daffodils.

Next year, we'll recall
how the sky, empty of airplanes,
revealed to us the birds,
the two-throated
note we'd forgotten.

The Season of the Hawk

A sparrowhawk fell
in front of our cracked cement steps,
Warren Street just west of bright blue

J. Michaels Furniture Store, sued
In 1972 for selling shoddy goods on credit
to poor New Yorkers.

We took him in,
shared boiled eggs and toast,
let him hop-fly our three rooms. He grew

weary of it all as his bird-ankle healed
and we drove him upstate
to feed on smaller birds.

Only a stray feather, scrabbling marks on the sill,
proved how close we had come to wildness.

Ballet Slippers

we wore inside and out
barely touched the ground.

Those were the sex-everywhere-
but-in-the-bedroom years
when we were sky-high

and never looked down.
Then we blinked
and there were children

to feed and pick up and we couldn't
get enough of their scent, the balled fists
gripping our fingers. We buckled

them in, hauled them all over. Sure,
we mourned the earth-skimming
untethered years but what

if we had missed
this steady gravitational pull
this insistent ground?

Dharma Talk

for Tuesday night sangha

Sit with it, sit into
it. Let the long bones
of your cramped thighs
drop onto the cushion. If they throb,
let them, breathe with them.
Shuddering, ragged
sounds. You could let
your mind fly out
the window straight across
the trash bins overflowing
with limp pizza boxes,
into the grimy bus stop glass
smeared with teen-age
love notes in breath-
drawn hearts,
where someone else
is just trying to breathe
her tired way home.

My Mother's Girl

On foot, just a block
north of Momo's Market,
the shriek of tires snaps me
from my mind-blank thoughts—
a guy driving too fast, too close
to a woman walking
on the other side
of the street. Her slack face tells
she is no stranger to his rage.
The arc of his spittle
catches in the fading light.
"*That's all I wanted to do*," he yells,
but, it's not. Back in the car,
he follows her, speeds up, brakes again,
inches from her small body.

I am back
on 86th Street in Brooklyn,
my mother screaming up
at an open window,
a man's arm raised. *I know*
what you're doing to her.
I'm not leaving until you stop.

And he did stop, that day.
Why should I be surprised
30 years later
to hear myself, her daughter,
yell, too?

Snow Storm in Quarantine

Wet wool on radiators
evokes every winter classroom

you knew, that smell
as much animal as plant

next to boots that give up
puddles, maps to countries

you meant to explore.

Dull-edged scraping of metal on asphalt.
Our muted street.

Interview

When was the first time
you betrayed someone?
Could it have
been done another way?
What did the words let loose?
Did writing the poem bring
anguish or relief—a torrent
of tears or a long-held scream?
On a scale of one to ten:
Was the release closer
to sneeze or orgasm?
Both at once?
Did the betrayee(s) ever
find out? How
did she/they react? Were you
forgiven? Was the poem worthy
of the sin? the sin
worthy of the poem?
Would you do it again?

Wedding Statistics

At our table of six, we can claim
enough ex-partners
to staff a start-up, field
a team. The bride has hand-lettered
place cards, secured them
with found scallop shells

leaving no evidence that the history
she emerges from—a girlhood divided
among many households—
marks her as *high risk*.

The groom's father toasts to a family
that does not believe in divorce
and leaves a good half
of us feeling slapped.
This starts to feel
like America, and we're trapped
in some swing state, the polls
still hours from closing, everything
riding on the outcome.

We carry the flowers home
like contestants who didn't win
but showed up and fought hard.
Goldenrod and rosa rugosa
gathered at dawn by the bride.
No professional would have risked
these fractious combinations.

Final Session

I. What I Say

I let him know—he of the 45-minute
hour—that he taught me intimacy
comes packaged with conflict. Can't love
if you can't fight. The trick
is to love clean,
not fight dirty.

I do not tell him
I am not wholly cured
but okay enough to trudge
back out every day,
a warrior who keeps her weapons
in good repair and within reach.

I do not squander bullets.
Though I have fewer
reasons to go to war, I would
kill for them, not talk.
It would be over
in less than three-quarters of an hour.

II. What I Don't

I was never tempted
to seduce you.
Too bland, too blond,
too interested in my weekly review
of shortcomings.
Your advice full sentences.
I like incomplete, half-constructed
throw-away, take-it-or-leave-it
asides. If you're bored,

show me. If you like my legs,
go there. You never even looked
when my blouse buttons pulled
as I reached for the tissues,
didn't ask if I would stay
with him or come back
for another session.

What's Your Favorite Tool and Why?

I settle on a humble
pair of scissors, having loved them
since the clumsy days
of rounded tips and ragged seams.
That power to split
one thing into two, keep going
until squares became strips
became confetti, then fairy dust.

That power to make invisible bits
of silk thread disappear,
turn what I had made
into something finer.
The silky *shh-shh*
of elegant separation
with intention.

Then I remembered
the delete key, a kind
of tool, one simple
stroke to erase the words
I almost sent, the cliché
you were saved from
but I can't help loving.

Both tools give
a chance
to start again:
cut out a tongue
or slash a heart into halves.

Blues

We could learn to love
this stillness. Nothing
worth driving to.
Whatever the pantry holds
is good and all
that is necessary.
Some evenings it is enough
that the blue
recycling barrel
lays down its perfect
angled shadow,
that every sock released
from the dryer, crackling
with static, has a mate.

II.

She Does Not Forget

the dead, sends notes
to the right people
at the correct times,

loves the tradition
of the Yahrzeit candle,
its long, steady burn.

On anniversaries for grieving
she holds a small tin
of ashes, her mother's,

a map of the cemetery
where her grandmother
was buried sixty years ago.

But she forgets, now and then,
exactly *who* is dead,
which friends are orphans,

whose parent
she already sat for
or worse, whose memorial

she attended, for whom she wept
in the black umbrella cold.

Sledding Hills I Have Known

Wooden deck, metal runners
whetted to weapon-grade sharpness
children and sleds dropped off
by a parent in a rush
thrilled to land inches
from Sunrise Highway
close enough to feel
the two-door two-tone
sedans whiz by, the drivers
not even looking at us.
Is it always this cold here?
my South Carolina sister asks
20 years later, sliding
on a Vermont hill.
Our kids zipped into five layers
join the cartoonish others
knocked off their feet
by runaway sleds, unleashed dogs.
We watch as our now ex-husbands
smash down on their tailbones
both of them limping, sitting
for six months on heating pads.
Sleds have turned into
saucers and tubes. A sea
of popsicle pinks and blue-greens,
colors that didn't used to be.
Dads stand by to record
or rescue. It is not
that we love our children more
than in the wooden sled days,
but we have found
so many new words

for danger.

Black Ice

High-pitched aria
of exquisite pain,
sight narrowed

to a sidewalk crack.
Just a wrist, no big deal.
I am already heroic.

Ahead: a wrench-shaped
titanium implant, three
dwarf-like screws.

*You'll get so much
writing done,* a friend says.
Instead, I fled to Netflix,

tracked down every British
police procedural, became an expert
on the Crown's judicial system.

There are a hundred broken wrist stories,
mostly women's, almost all on ice,
many involving leashed dogs.

Here's one: A much younger woman
in a full-on slam to the ground
after a night at the bars,

her two wrists snapped
as easily as wishbones
three days after Thanksgiving.

I envied
her chance to heal twice,
her better story.

Unable to manage,
double-casted,
she had to cut her wild,

gorgeous curls, ten years
of tumbling hip-length beauty.
Her hair grew back. Her wrists mended.

Beginning with A

an axe to grind
a bed to weed

a bone to pick
a cheek to turn

a fence to mend
a plate to crack

a rock to wear
around your neck

a life: this one
to claim.

Prodigal

Gas tank empty
car seats drenched in snow-melt
from wide-open window driving,
I return home, hours late.
First Christmas I'm no longer
in full-time residence.
Slipping up the stairs, wine-soaked
breath, hair witchy with wind,
I think *We are done here*
uncertain what I mean by
done
or *here* or *we*.

Now, Then

This woman bent forward
over her walker
wearing canary boxing shorts—
I am the nutty one
in fuzzy red stick-on letters
straggling across her broad behind—
jets me back to those bad
boys from the middle school years,
sneaking up to tape *Kick Me*
notes to the backs of
the quiet hunched kids
who brought slim paper bags
from home. We who bought lunch
were just one shaky rung
higher on this slick ladder—
thirty-five cents
for overcooked beef
in oozy brown liquid.
It was never good, never
tasted of anything.

No Martha, No Mary

At best a reluctant cook, furious
housekeeper, anything living
or not, fair game
when the vacuum cleaner
roared. Four children,

a house clean
as a miniature
model home
might have fooled you, but she
was in the wrong era, wrong
marriage, wrong life.

No Madonna
of the downcast eyes,
in an ill-fitting blue wrap,
only angels at a gaping tomb
to talk to in the end.

A good hand of bridge
made my mother
come alive, as did the days
after the plows came by
and we kids went back to school.

Funk and Wagnalls Standard Encyclopedia

Each page was edged with gold leaf.
$2.99 added to the grocery bill.

We grew terrified of skipping a volume—
missing, say, FAL-GRO—

leaving a family-sized gap
in our knowledge

of famines, Florida,
getaways or Greek ruins.

My mother aimed to fill a shelf
as we made our way slowly,

afraid to learn too much but starting
to love the world we'd yet to see from

our small house, its walls porous enough
to put a man-sized fist through.

In that same determined way
my mother built

a collection of Melmac dishware,
week by week, piece by piece.

"Look," she'd say
before shaking out our morning corn flakes,

pouring milk. "It's called Dusty
Rose. See how the inside glows."

When the New Rink Opened

My mother's skates were holdovers
from the days when her high school yearbook

named her Miss Happy-Go-Lucky.
And for a nano-second

I saw it, the corners of her eyes lifted,
a mittened hand raised high.

She glided by, away
from us. My father, ridiculous

in blood red earmuffs,
all of us mismatched in wet wool.

We skated just that once
and it was enough.

On the drive home we cried
as our feet thawed, but we had chipped

that sharp ice with our dull blades,
etched small cracks on the glaze.

Safe as Houses

Post-war, three-rooms
on stilts. Two rickety flights
of outdoor steps stood shakily between
me and the back-from-the Pacific dads,
lined up in hip boots along
the white surf. In formation,
they cast long, bamboo rods.

Awake too early from a nap,
I leaned and called out
and fell, though I know this
only from family lore. No scars
give evidence. What I can call up
from those days of improvised housing

are the hermit crabs
scuttling for their lives
through cement gray sand,
in ill-fitting shells
left behind by mollusks
and the tinkling silver suck
of water receding,
returning, leaving again.

On Being Asked to Write a Poem for Peace

for my parents

What I know of war is swiped
from cracked film and photos, stills
of a khaki-clad guy, neatly shaved, held tight
by a girl ready to dance, a girl whisked

from the steno pool, assigned
this night to the role of light company, a treat
for the man who walked into her life
and for an evening they are young.

I still have those snapshots. Stunned
is how they look to me—
not knowing what they've done.

I Would Kill For You

my mother swore
more than once.
She did not lay praise

on flawed essays,
over-reliant
on the passive voice,
or tedious art projects

whose golden
macaroni bits
didn't last
the bus ride home.

Did she know even then
we would never
need her to murder
for us, hoist a car

from our crushed bodies,
brave the space between all
and nothing
in her slim sundress,
her lovely bare arms?

We Were Not Good Dog People

My mother held Peppy (or was it Mike?)
too loosely by his collar
the day Wayne Porter showed up,
asking my brother to play.

The storm door shattered
as our boxer flew through.
Wayne, stunned by the speed and noise,
trails of blood streaming down his face.

It's not as bad as it looks,
our mother told his an hour later.
No stitches,
no lawsuits. Maybe it was time

to switch to the screen door anyway.
This story was one my father
laughed at. The kid, after all, wasn't his,
wasn't hurt, the dog came back, the door repaired.

But my mother and I
had seen a child bloodied
and stunned into silence,
a dog take flight through a door.

The Neighbors' Ground Cover

We lived in square, shingled houses
called *starters* with our fathers
back from war.
We'd see them
stare over the backyards,
playgrounds, the train tracks
circling to work and home.

Everyone planted grass, sprayed it
for a lethal green hue.
But the Kinzies planted portulaca—
unruly colors, best left untended—
while their boys built things
with grown-up tools, taught us
to dam creeks with sticks.

At my mother's second wedding—
the green metal rakes discarded,
starter houses long finished— we watched
our unencumbered neighbors
dance closer
than any couple on the floor.

On the Platform

Along the slab of iron track
we lined up our bottle money

dimes, a few pennies
to test their copper,

along the slab of iron track
minutes before the train pulled in.

My grandmother, shifting her still-warm
bag of leftovers, waved us

back from the raging engine
as the tracks began to shake

and the train shrieked to a halt.
We saw coins fly between tracks,

hurried our grandmother up the steps,
waved her back to Brooklyn, stayed there

long enough to duck the hot exhaust,
tore back out to the tracks

to find our flattened money
had turned into something

other than currency:
thin as eye slits,

fingernail clippings,
waning crescent moons.

Toward Resurrection

At eight I hated
Easter— its half-hearted shade

of barely-there pink, receding
as it preens; itchy dresses,

useless straw hats, elastic
strings to hold them in place

as if we were little Dorothys
waiting for a tornado.

I would never
be a pastel girl

although I could
make my way

on the sidelines, bide
my time until the late buses

left, the sky magenta before turning black
as the stone rolled back.

Not Our First

We'd had old people die,
but this felt like our first "real" death—
the one we could not stop
repeating at the bus stop,
scuffing our gym sneakers
until they lost their white.
I can't believe Mr. Crockett is dead.
How the neighborhood turned carnival
that night, sirens screaming
through the intersection of Schermerhorn
and Willis, kids and parents
in pajamas sprung from beds
running in that still summer air
to a spectacle of light and noise.
Our first not-that-old person.
A heart attacked
by death. Our first kid
friend without a parent.
He was not our favorite
neighborhood dad, bellowing
from the porch for his kids
to come in before dark
while the rest of us captured the flag.
But still: A death! Dead.
Nothing to do with grief.

I Thought I Had Remembered Everything

until my sister said, *I still see Dad*
pushing Mom down the stairs.
How had I missed that violation,
its wormwood memory?

My father was the kind of guy who took
his kids to the old-fashioned
ice cream place, each cone
dipped deep in hardening chocolate

who cried when we won ribbons
at the third-rate horse shows,
had our names in the paper
for honor roll.
Who called his mother-in-law *Mom*.

Was ours still dressed
from work in her pencil skirt
and tucked-in blouse
looking like a woman working
her way up? More likely,
she was in a nightgown and sashed
poly robe, about to lose
another night's sleep.

Two Wheels

for Chris

Daring where I was wary,
first in all things
bold and animal,
my younger sister
ran for our mother.
I, on my two-wheeler
had mastered finally,
balance, coasting,
but not braking. I still taste
the day I circled and circled
the block, a minor moon
in her orbit.

I had wanted
my mother's gaze
and even late, distracted,

it still counts.

No God Would Have Let a Man

bruise her cheek, break her rib,
fall to his knees in apology,
swear *never again*.

My mother was no longer a believer
but she let Carlos, part-time pastor,
perform her second marriage
in dove-white vestments

hands high in full-faith
celebration. That day
we all believed

in second or third
chances, if not forgiveness.
We wrapped ourselves around

each other and danced
as if there were no yesterday.

III.

Settling the Estate

The unwritten rule
between my siblings and me
declared if you had given the gift,
it came back to you

as if you were always
the intended heir. I became owner
of a porcelain bowl

I had coveted, even as I gave it
to our mother long after
she stopped desiring
such things. I was counting on beauty,

however fragile, to keep her alive.

A Little Light

You are erasing all evidence of him,
the younger sister accuses,
wiping away signs of the father
who let the phone go dead,
cancelled Christmas,
lived too long alone
inside the drapes-drawn house.

I am making room
the older one, spray bottle raised,
replies, giving him the space
he always wanted
to sift through stacks
of old <u>Scientific Americans</u>,
archived since before Pluto
was diminished to dwarf status

until he found just the article
he meant to show you, *letting in*
a little light, too.

The Reading

For Lydia Davis

What inspires you? The visiting writer
twists her hammered silver
bracelets, tries not to check the time.

She has been generous beyond
her agreed-on stipend.
Small fatigue lines

show in the low five p.m.
November light. A ruder guest
would answer *How could you not know?*

She has just read entire stories
of only three lines,
whole, not fragments.

One could have been
about two students in the back row,

quietly tracing each other's tattoos.

American Music

I. Pee Wee

She listens hard
while the sax hesitates; light tympani
from the back, flick
of brush against metal.
The pianist handpicks the notes
as if choosing pears,
going for ripe, not too soft,
yellow, trace of rose.
And everyone else
at this dinner plate-
sized table fades,
the sound of their breathing
almost too much
to bear.

II. Jazz Lady Speaks, Finally

We never played the same
piece we practiced

but you had to be there,
had to know what

you were turning
your back on

and how: aching
with regret

at betraying
some guy's music

or in anger,
screaming my turn, *finally,*

or in sadness:
you didn't mean to

abandon the old ways.
Honestly.

III. Lost in the Music, Lost in the City

Can she trust
the wandering bass
to carry her home,
ease her back down
to the place she left?
Or is this just another
half-seduction:
Follow me, follow me.
No promises.

IV. Take it or Leave it

The nursing mother
in the Coldplay t-shirt
feels her breasts let down,
weep cool and sticky
when the guys on the roof
start to play their horns.
So hot the windows steam
on both sides, air wet
enough to suck through a straw.
Flecks of loose paint

rusty and sharp
catch on bare feet.
Jet black on the wire,
crows hold themselves
as if listening, wings
too slow and heavy to open.

The Sunday Dads

At the park, they watch
their children closely—only the briefest
side-eyes at their phones—

sips of that other
world as they stand
ready for what won't

likely happen on their watch,
not even a pink scrape.
In the museums

these same fathers move
gallery to gallery
alert as the uniformed monitors.

They snap photos discreetly.
"Did you see that one?"
they ask the children,

sensitive to the women artists,
invisible for too long,
their work found

in attics and flea markets
a hundred years after death.
The fathers are making up for omissions.

The *Yes, Dear* Wife

Of course
you ate guinea pig
in Peru, I confirm,
biked twelve miles
in the blinding rain
to score fresh
bluefish at sunset
when the boats came in,
called your mother,
wrote the children,
paid quarterly taxes
even before
they were due, found
that small vintage pinot noir
we had almost given up on.
If I squint, I still see
rose-tinged circles bleeding
on the table cloth,
trace their perfect rings.

Canal Street Station

Not a rape
not even an assault
just a generic subway rider staring
at the dark, smudged window
while he rubbed against my
pole-gripping hand,
my butter yellow leather glove
from Century 21,
before my mind caught up
and figured this was not
just a crowded Monday rush.
On the platform my clean
trembling left hand
peeled the right-hand glove
down to the tips, sneaked it
into the lipstick-stained
coffee cup overflowing metal
bin. The lie at the ready:
*It didn't happen. It
was nothing.*

The Bargain

My mother did her part,
made sure we had
clean, folded gym clothes
on Monday. Checked
and signed our homework.

In turn, we kids
washed and rinsed
nightly dishes, ignoring
her bruised cheeks, pale

mauve, lilac, her grimace
as she took a breath. We wiped
the dishes quietly,
left them clean

but not polished enough
to see our reflections.

The Only Girl at the Ring

in black patent leather shoes
buckled at the ankles, grosgrain bows
at the throat. The run-down
horse stable offered $2.00
riding lessons and my mother,
child of the Depression,
couldn't turn down
what she'd never known.

I'd been told to show up
in leather-soled shoes
and these—aside from gym sneakers—
were all I had.
the instructor asked,
Do you always
ride a horse
in church shoes?
I shrugged.
Let them outride me,
knew I could outrun them.

Leavetaking

For Jonah

What starts as a story
of addition
and expansion
becomes a ritual
of leaving. No one warned us
that loss is more, not less.
Like those wagons
in *Little House on the Prairie*
carving deeper ruts as they pull
the new family
to the new house
in the new land. We wave
our faded bits of cloth,
grow smaller with your steady
progress away from us. We
are the ones
who disappear.

Things I Think About in the Dark

What became of the girls
who slipped switchblades
down their boot shafts
before they left for the late shift
at the all-night Quickie Mart?

On the school bus,
I watched my seatmate
write, *Don't be Cruel*
in permanent marker on her arm.
I was too awestruck to look hard,
but I saw her perfect cat's-eye
liner, caught her spearmint scent.
They didn't just smoke, those bold
girls. Their parents *allowed them* to.

About the rest of their lives
we knew nothing:
so scared of walking to our cars
in dark lots, we timid ones kept
to our babysitting
routines, let ourselves
be driven home at two a.m.
by the too-friendly, boozy-breathed
buddies of our parents asking us,
at every turn, for direction.

I Am Done

hoarding white linen
steam-pressed for dinner guests.
Done with *good* clothes,
dry-clean-only sparkly
things that make me tug
my gut in, say no to chocolate
mousse. Finished with stashing
the expensive bottle of red
from the vineyard we swore
we would rediscover.
Which birthday, graduation
retirement, five-year anniversary
of the last chemo treatment
would we celebrate?

Share it with the next
neighbors who walk up the drive
to return a rake or the Fed Ex guy
who delivers something
you could have lived without.
Suck your way
into that plunging
sequined item and wipe
his red-stained mouth
on monogrammed damask.

ACKNOWLEDGMENTS AND GRATITUDE

"American Music" appeared under a different title and in an earlier version in River Arts Online and *Green Mountains Review* published "Wedding Statistics," "When the Girls Were Girls," and "A Little Light." "I Told Myself I was Done," "Interview" and "No God Would Have Let a Man" appeared in *Meat for Tea: The Valley Review*. "Our Silent Spring" is forthcoming in *Tupelo Quarterly*. "I Would Kill for You" appeared in *Barrow Street*.

"Funk and Wagnalls Standard Encyclopedia" and "Not Our First" are included in *Roads Taken: Contemporary Vermont Poetry*, Third Edition.

I am grateful to Vermont Studio Center for time and support and the Ruth Stone House for honoring poets who live in the full, demanding world of work and family.

This book needed to grow and change before it took the shape it did. It would not have drawn breath without the writers and readers in my life. Thank you Warren Wilson MFA community, Ghita Orth, Rebecca Starks, and Nancy Mitchell, especially, who has been my touchstone, my lighthouse, my evening and morning stars. I thank my friends who have kept me whole and writing, the Ospreys who have lifted me up, Dan for never doubting the power of writing, Tim for technical support that made sure the poems and I didn't spin off into space. Deep thanks to the vision and sustained commitment of Gloria Mindock, editor and guide, and Allison O'Keefe who turned this manuscript into a book.

For my siblings, Christine, Brian, and Joan, my first and always crew. For my children, Jonah, Amy, Emily, Chris and Margaret, my beloveds, through birth and marriage and sheer divine intervention.

ABOUT THE AUTHOR

Barbara E. Murphy's poetry has appeared or is forthcoming in journals including *Green Mountains Review*, *Threepenny Review*, *Barrow Street*, and *New England Review*. She is a recipient of a Vermont Arts Council Fellowship and twice-nominated for a Pushcart Prize. Murphy served as a faculty member at the New England Young Writers Conference and is a board member of Sundog Poetry. A collection of her poems, <u>Almost Too Much</u> was published by Cervena Barva Press in 2015.

Her essays and reviews have been published in several venues including *The New York Times*, *Plume Poetry*, *Full Grown People*, and *Green Mountains Review*. She lives and writes in Burlington Vermont.

Printed in the USA
CPSIA information can be obtained
at www.ICGtesting.com
CBHW021139200824
13376CB00026B/159

9 781950 063925